A Circle
of Smiles

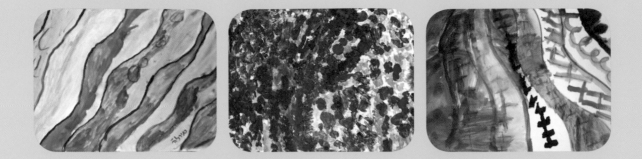

This book is dedicated in memory of Kerrie E. Slater. With deep appreciation to family and friends and with special thanks to Julie and Paul Candau who made the publication possible.

This book is a reality because of one truly amazing person, Amy Slater-Ovadia. With understanding, acceptance and love for all, and incredible passion, Amy has worked tirelessly for the Children of Beit Issie Shapiro both in Israel and the United States as a long time staff member. Her many accomplishments were the result of a strong will and a relentless dedication to make change. With all our hearts, and on behalf of the children and families of Beit Issie Shapiro, we thank Amy for all that she has done.

Sylvia Rouss is the award-winning author of the Sammy Spider series. She is a teacher at the Early Childhood Center at Stephen S. Wise Temple. Sylvia received the National Jewish Book award for The Littlest Pair and Sydney Taylor awards for Tali's Jerusalem Scrapbook, Sammy Spider's First Shavuot, and Sammy Spider's First Trip to Israel. She has over 30 books in print. Sylvia is a featured author and lecturer at book fairs throughout the United States and Israel.

You can learn more about Sylvia by visiting www.sylviarouss.com

Library of Congress Cataloging-in-Publication Data

Rouss, Sylvia A.
    A circle of smiles : a story about Beit Issie Shapiro, Israel's leading organization in the field of disability / by Sylvia Rouss.
       p.   cm.
    ISBN 978–0–9829273–1–1 (pbk. : alk. paper)
    1. Beit Issie Shapiro–Juvenile literature. 2. People with disabilities–Services for–Israel–Juvenile literature. I. Title.
HV1559.I75R68 2011
362.3095694–dc22   2010039650

Manufactured in the United States of America
1 – CG – 12/31/10

A Circle of Smiles

A story about Beit Issie Shapiro,
Israel's leading organization in
the field of disability

By Sylvia Rouss

בית איזי שפירא
לשינוי באיכות חייהם של אנשים עם מוגבלויות

Beit Issie Shapiro
Changing the lives of people with disabilities

בקמפוס וילי וסיליה טראמפ
On the Willie & Celia Trump Campus

"Wake up, Rachel." I hear my mommy's voice calling.

"It's Cycles for Smiles day!"

"Yippee!" I shout. Today I will ride a tricycle at my school to raise money for a school in Israel called Beit Issie Shapiro. Some people just call it Beit Issie.

It is where my cousin, Yoni, goes to school. Next week my family will fly to Israel to see my mommy's brother, Uncle Dave and his wife, Aunt Talia, and Yoni. We will bring the money from Cycles for Smiles and give it to Beit Issie. I can hardly wait to visit Yoni and see his school. The last time I was in Israel, I was two and I don't remember much about that trip. Now I am four years old, just like Yoni.

"Cycles For Smiles" is part of our milestones Programming at American Friends of Beit Issie Shapiro, which introduces children to "their" buddy in Israel, teaches that everyone has abilities and disabilities, educates about special needs, creates a connection to beautiful Israel, and teaches that "i" can make a difference at any age.

This morning we left for Israel. Yoni and my aunt and uncle are meeting us at the airport. I've seen lots of pictures of my cousin. His legs don't work like mine so he has a special chair called a wheelchair that helps him get around.

When I finally see Yoni, I smile at him and he smiles back. Everyone around us is speaking Hebrew and I don't know what they are saying. My mommy told me that Yoni doesn't speak, but his teachers at Beit Issie have taught him how to use his hands and face to talk to others. I guess it's like me not being able to speak Hebrew. I smile and wave at everyone to let them know that I am happy to see them. Because Yoni is smiling too, I think he is happy to see us.

The next day I wake up before Mommy and Daddy. I tiptoe to the kitchen where my Aunt Talia is helping Yoni eat breakfast. Yoni's hands can't hold a spoon but I see him raise his hand just a little when he looks at me. I wave back as my aunt taps the chair next to her. My aunt is Israeli and she only speaks Hebrew. I guess she wants me to sit down and have breakfast. Yoni and I smile at each other the whole time because we are glad to be together.

Finally, we leave for Beit Issie. It's just a short distance from Yoni's house. Aunt Talia pushes Yoni in his wheelchair while I walk. She lets me take a turn pushing Yoni and finally we arrive at his school. Yoni's teacher, Mira, greets us with a "Boker Tov!" She speaks a little English and she asks, "Rachel would you like to see the school?"

"Yes," I nod.

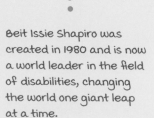

Beit Issie Shapiro was created in 1980 and is now a world leader in the field of disabilities, changing the world one giant leap at a time.

We start in Yoni's classroom where Mira introduces me to Yoni's friends. Some are in wheelchairs like Yoni and some are not. They all smile at me and a few say my name. I think they like me. The classroom has toys and books like mine but there is more space to move around. One of Yoni's friends is celebrating her birthday and her whole family is there! Her grandpa is taking pictures while her parents and grandma help blow out the candles on her cake.

After meeting Yoni's friends, we go to the playground. It looks a lot like the playground at my school but it has some things that my school doesn't. I happily clap my hands when I see the swings and Mira asks if I would like to play on them. I get on and then I see that there is a way to attach Yoni's wheelchair so that he can swing, too. Yoni and I laugh as Mira pushes both of us. The playground has lots of fun things to do and it is built so that Yoni can use it just like me.

Park Chaverim is a magical playground where children of all abilities can live, laugh... and play! The first disability-friendly playground in Israel promoting, friendship and inclusion.

Then Mira takes us to the sports room. It's like the gym where my mommy and daddy go except this one is for kids. I try to climb a wall that has places for my hands and feet. "Whoops!" I yell as I slip and fall onto a soft mat. Yoni looks worried but when I start laughing, he laughs too.

Next, we go to the pool. I wait as Mira puts on Yoni's swimsuit and takes him into the water without his wheelchair. She tells me that the water helps him move his body. She points to the water and asks, "Rachel, do you want to come in, too?" I shake my head and sit on the edge of the pool. Yoni moves his arms while Mira holds him. Suddenly, Yoni splashes me and we both giggle.

Beit Issie Shapiro was the first in Israel to provide Hydrotherapy (water therapy.) Water gives children with disabilities a gift to move more freely and a chance to control their bodies which makes them feel good and have loads of fun!

After leaving the pool, we go to the "Snoezelen room." I think that is a very funny name and there is nothing like it at my school. The room is dark and quiet. I hold onto Yoni's hand because I'm a little scared. But then I see beautiful lights all around me and lots of colored bubbles. I pretend that we are under the ocean. I'm a mermaid princess and Yoni is the king sitting on his throne.

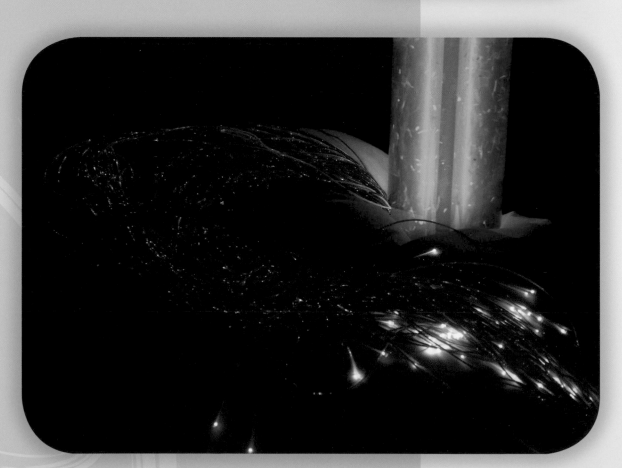

Snoezelen is a magical setting with a mixture of sights, sounds, touches, and smells. Everyone who goes in to explore are curious about what will happen. It makes a huge difference in the life of everyone who spends time there. Always searching for innovative ways to make a difference, Beit Issie Shapiro brought Snoezelen to Israel.

A little later, we walk by a dentist office.
I'm very surprised because there isn't a dentist
at my school. As we peer through a window,
Mira says, "See the parpar, Rachel? It helps
children feel safe." I don't know what a parpar is
but then I see a child wrapped up in the wings
of a big beautiful butterfly. My dentist doesn't
have a parpar. I wish he did.

Beit Issie Shapiro is
the first in the world to
"snoezel" the dental clinic
which has the wonderful
result of soothing patients.

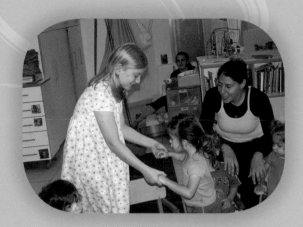

Beit Issie Shapiro
classrooms are created
with "special" in mind! Lots
and lots of room to play
and learn and everybody
is welcome to visit. When
are you coming?

Finally we end up back in Yoni's classroom. My mommy is there to pick me up. I run to her, "Mommy," I shout. "I love Yoni's school!"

"I'm glad you had a good time," she says. Then she gives me the envelope with the money from Cycles for Smiles. "This will help Beit Issie continue to be such a good school," she tells me.

Mira has taken Yoni to join his friends in a circle. Excitedly, I dash over and give her the envelope. She hugs me and says, "Todah rabbah, thank you!" I look at Yoni and his friends and I feel very happy because I see a "circle of smiles" looking back at me.

Ideas for Educators and Parents

1. Rachel uses gestures and facial expressions to communicate in the story because she doesn't speak Hebrew. Ask the children in your class to try "speaking" without using words.

2. Use "expression cards" and see if children can identify the feelings depicted.

3. Have children share what is special about themselves.

4. Have children discuss how they are the same as their peers and how they are different.

5. Have children talk about how they feel when they go to the dentist. Ask children why they think the parpar helps children feel safe when they visit the dentist.

6. Ask children how they could help their friends eat if they couldn't use their hands.

7. Discuss with children how their body feels when they are in a swimming pool. Ask how they move their body in the swimming pool.

8. Yoni uses a wheelchair to get around. Ask children in what ways, besides walking, they can move around (eg., tricycle, stroller, scooter, bouncy ball, swimming, crawling).

9. How is your school like Beit Issie Shapiro and how is it different?

10. Ask children which part of Beit Issie Shapiro is their favorite?